To my Guardian of Light, find your passion,

then your quest will be clear.

Published in association with Bear With Us Productions.

© 2024 My Dad Does PR
Dan Turk

The right of Dan Turk as the author of this work has been asserted by him in accordance with the Copyright Designs and Patents Act 1988.
All rights reserved, including the right of reproduction in whole or part in any form.

ISBN Paperback: 979-8-8707-3435-4
ISBN Hardback: 979-8-8691-9971-3

www.justbearwithus.com

MY DAD DOES PR

WRITTEN BY
DAN TURK

ILLUSTRATED BY
YEVHENIIA LISOVA

In a bustling city, so tall and grand,
Went a little girl named **Sofia**, hand in hand,
With her **dad** to work, a great mystery,
A job she knew he had, but what it was, she couldn't quite see.

He wasn't

A dentist,
Mailman,
Or cook,

She only knew that **lots of meetings** he took.
Typing away, or **talking** on calls,
When he 'did PR', Dad gave his all.

On that sunny day, they stepped into an elevator.
Up they went, Sofia and her dad, along with a stranger.
A question was asked, fluttering so free:
"What does your dad do?" asked the stranger, you see.

Sofia looked up with a curious smile.
"**I'm not quite sure**, to explain may take a while.
He talks to people, helps them understand,
But how he does it, I can't quite command."

With a **wink** and a **chuckle**, her dad began,
"To tell you what I do, let's hatch a plan,
We'll go to my office, and learn all about it,
From pictures and papers, and so many products."

"To start, you should know, **I work with many a story**,
Helping companies share ideas in all of their glory.
Big, medium, or small, it matters not a bit,
If they make cool stuff, I tell everyone about it."

"Imagine," he said, "**a magical thread**
Connecting thoughts in each person's head.
I weave those threads to create a tale,
About gadgets and devices that help people prevail."

They entered his office, a big room filled with light.
Sofia's eyes sparkled. **"Oh, Miami, what a sight!"**
She looked at the pictures and products and spinning seat,
Dancing as she explored, to the office's musical beat.

"See this picture here," said her dad,
"Of these **earbuds**?" "How cool!"

"I helped tell this story,
And used every tool!"

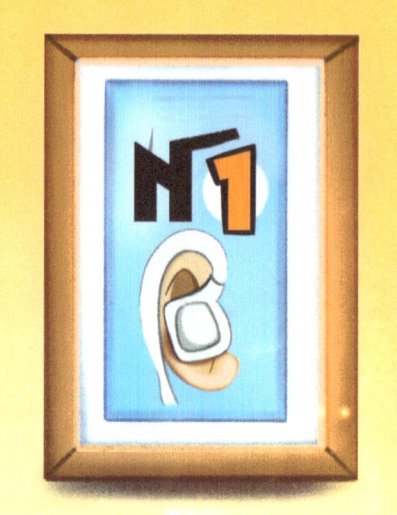

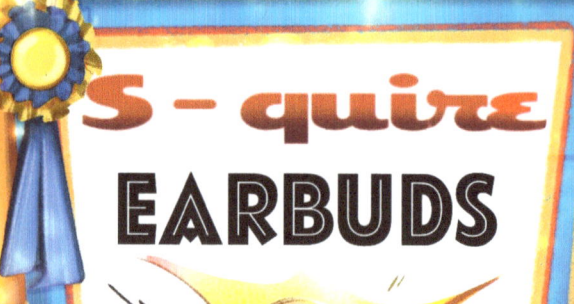

"You see, some people can't hear as well as you or me,
But these earbuds are special,
Helping everyone hear, like glasses help us see."

"Not everyone knew such earbuds existed,
But **together**, with my team, **we persisted**.
We worked on the story until it was just right,
Then shared it with people who helped it take flight."

Sofia nodded, beginning to see
The threads of her dad's work, **Just like a bee.**

Buzzing and busy, **spreading the word**,
Through stories, like this one, that made people feel heard.

They talked, they laughed, what fun they had,
On their **daddy-daughter date**, both **happy** and **glad**.
At his office Sofia learned her dad's special skill
Was creating and sharing stories. "Oh, what a thrill!

One more thing occurred to Sofia that day,
A realization, in a very special way;
Not every job, like her dad's, was easy to explain,
But each was important, like an engine to a plane.

Her dad's work with stories, big, medium, and small,
Showed that each job and its worker had a unique call
To make a difference, in their own ways,
Brightening the world, like the sun's warm rays.

As they left the office, hand in hand once more,
Sofia felt proud, inspired to her core.
She had learned a lesson, so simple but true,
About jobs, about work, about what people do.

So, for all the boys and girls just like Sofia,
Who go to their parents' work, here's a reminder for ya–

Learn about their jobs, their passions, their quests,

**So you can proudly share what they do,
When next put to the test.**

Milton Keynes UK
Ingram Content Group UK Ltd.
UKHW021658220324
439743UK00011B/36